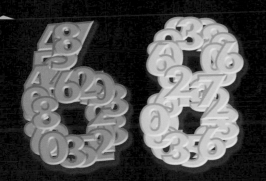

68 Ways to Save the Planet Before Bedtime

Paul Mason

CONTENTS

Sending Out an S.O.S   2

Make Friends with a Spider   4

Wear Fewer Clothes   6

Make Your Granny Happy   8

Don't Just Stand By   10

Waste Not, Want Not   12

Make a Monstrous Sock   14

See the World by Bike!   16

Love a Library   18

Be a Role Model   20

Think Differently   22

Glossary and Index   24

SENDING OUT AN S.O.S.

Planet Earth is an amazing place. Just look around at the plants and animals you can see. But Earth is in danger. Why? Well, because of us. Humans are always doing things that aren't good for the planet.

What's the problem?

Global warming is what we call the rise in the world's temperature. That might *sound* like a good thing, but even the smallest rise in temperature can have *big* effects on our planet.

Global warming causes:

- rising sea levels, which are bad for coastal areas
- changes in our weather, such as more extreme storms
- less food, because some of the world's farmland is becoming too dry to grow things

Sun

How global warming happens

1. Burning **fossil fuels such as** coal and oil releases **greenhouse gases**.

2. Greenhouse gases reach the **atmosphere**.

atmosphere

4. Heat is reflected back toward Earth.

3. Greenhouse gases trap heat.

Earth

Can we save the world?

Earth has a lot of resources, such as water, wood, food, and fossil fuels. These are very important to us, but we are using them up too quickly and they may not last.

Sounds scary, doesn't it? But don't worry! You can help to save the world—one small step at a time. Here are 68 ways how . . .

What can I do?

1 Start now

All you have to do is try one idea from this book before you go to bed today. What are you waiting for?

Top Tip!
This book is special—you can start reading wherever you want. So why not start in the middle?

3

MAKE FRIENDS WITH A SPIDER

How can spiders help save the world?

There's nothing a spider likes more than eating a load of tasty flies. So the next time you see a spider's web, be friendly and leave it there.

Spiders are an important part of the **food chain.** Without them there would be too many flies, and that would mean plants would not grow as well. But spiders get eaten too. Small birds love a tasty spider for lunch. It works like this:

Spiders eat flies.

Birds eat spiders, other insects, seeds, and fruit.

Spiders and birds are also part of other food chains.

The seeds come out in the birds' droppings.

Trees are perfect homes for spiders and birds.

The seeds grow into new plants and trees.

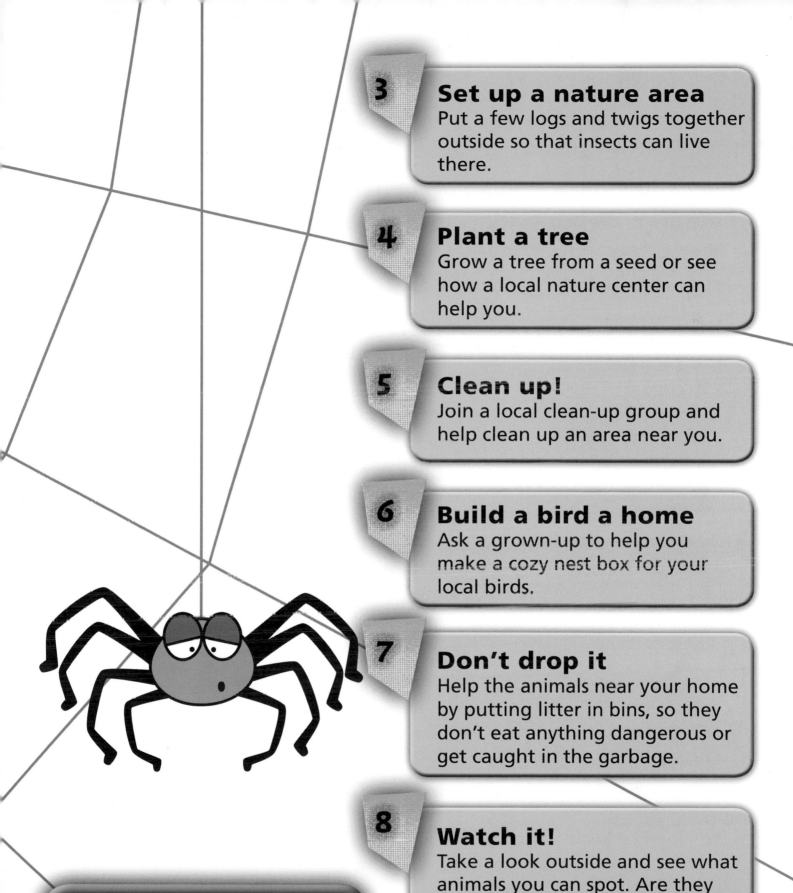

3 Set up a nature area
Put a few logs and twigs together outside so that insects can live there.

4 Plant a tree
Grow a tree from a seed or see how a local nature center can help you.

5 Clean up!
Join a local clean-up group and help clean up an area near you.

6 Build a bird a home
Ask a grown-up to help you make a cozy nest box for your local birds.

7 Don't drop it
Help the animals near your home by putting litter in bins, so they don't eat anything dangerous or get caught in the garbage.

8 Watch it!
Take a look outside and see what animals you can spot. Are they using your nature area or bird box? See ideas 3 and 6.

FAST FACT
Trees remove greenhouse gases from the air and make oxygen for us to breathe.

WEAR FEWER CLOTHES

No, this doesn't mean you have to walk around in your underwear to save the world! It really means "have fewer clothes in your closet." But hang on—how can that help?

How do clothes affect the world?

Everyone has a cotton T-shirt. But have you ever thought about what happens before that T-shirt ends up with you?

Growing the cotton
First, chemicals are used to grow and make cotton, which can be bad for the environment.

T-shirts do a lot of traveling . . .
The cotton has to go from the field to the mill and then to the factory to be made into a T-shirt.

. . . and then travel some more!
Even worse than that—many T-shirts are sold far from where they were made. You know what that means: **longer journeys = more greenhouse gases.**

So why not just have a couple of T-shirts you love rather than lots? See? Wear fewer clothes, and save the world!

FAST FACT
The chemicals used to grow and make cotton stay in the T-shirt.

10 **Stop growing?** Every now and again, your clothes will get too small. What a waste! But hang on—why not give them to charity?

11 **Look at the label** Get your mom or dad to look at the labels, and ask them to buy clothes made closer to home.

12 **Trade with friends** Bored with your clothes? Swap them with friends!

13 **Check out charity** You don't always have to buy new clothes. See what clothes you can find in a thrift shop.

14 **Wash less** Not you—your clothes! Some clothes don't need to be washed after every wear. Socks and pants probably do, though!

15 **Glasses give-away** Give your old glasses to a charity.

Top Tip!
Make sure your mom or dad knows what you're swapping or giving away.

7

MAKE YOUR GRANNY HAPPY

Make your granny happy *and* save the world? Sounds impossible, but it can be done. And it only takes a few seconds. On cold days, all you need to do is wear that sweater she knitted you.

How can sweaters save the world?

If your granny doesn't knit, don't worry. You can save the world with *any* sweater. Once you've got that lovely sweater on, you'll remember how warm it is. Then, persuade everyone else in your family to put a sweater on too. Notice anything? You're all really warm! Better turn down the heating.

Why turn off the heating?

The heating in many buildings uses electricity, which is usually made with fossil fuels, or gas, which *is* a fossil fuel.

So every time you turn down the heating, you help save the planet just a little bit.

Gas or electricity used for heating

Fossil fuels burned

Greenhouse gases released

Global warming

Top Tip!

Turning the heating down or off should be done by an adult.

17 Put on a hat
We lose lots of heat through our heads. Putting on a hat is a fast way to stay warm.

18 Toasty toes
Wear extra-thick socks to keep your toes happy.

19 Keep warm at night
Add an extra blanket to your bed.

20 Stop the draft
Shut doors and windows to keep rooms warm.

21 In place
Feeling cold? Try running in place. How do you feel now?

22 Hug your sister
It doesn't need to be your sister! Hug a friend or pet, and you'll soon feel warm.

23 DON'T JUST STAND BY

Who'd have thought you could save the world by flicking a switch? The switch you need is . . . the off switch! That's the *real* off switch, not the one that puts a device in "standby mode."

What's wrong with standby?

Lots of people turn things off using a standby button. The devices are not *really* off, because a little bit of electricity is still being used! Most of this electricity was made by burning fossil fuels. This produces greenhouse gases, which add to the greenhouse effect. When you *do* turn things off properly, they stop running completely.

> **less electricity wasted =**
> **fewer greenhouse gases**

Congratulations! With the flick of a switch, you've helped save the world!

Top Tip!
Check with a grown-up before turning things off. Not everything can be turned off. Refrigerators must stay on all the time!

24 Poster power
Design a poster to remind people to turn things off.

25 Start a "no-TV day"
For one day, turn the TV off and do something else instead.

26 Turn off the lights
But first make sure there's no one still in the room.

27 Think fast
Hungry? Don't stand with the refrigerator door open. Decide what you want and close it quickly.

28 Be bright
Get your parents to use energy-saving lightbulbs. They use less energy than others.

29 Summer sun
Dry your hair naturally when the weather is warm instead of using a hair dryer.

Want ideas for your no-TV day? See ideas 38 to 44.

WASTE NOT, WANT NOT

"Waste not, want not" means don't throw things away carelessly. Then you won't miss them later. It's the kind of thing your grandfather might say! "Wasting not" is also a good way to keep more garbage out of landfills.

What do we waste?

Every year, we throw away a mountain of garbage. In one year, Americans throw away about:

- 28 billion plastic bottles and jars
- 55 billion aluminum cans
- 200 million tons of garbage

Here are three things you can do to stop landfills from growing.

Reduce
Reduce the amount of waste you produce. Try to choose things that have little or no wrapping.

Recycle
If you must throw things away, put them in a recycling bin if possible.

Reuse
Try to reuse things instead of throwing them away.

31 Blow your nose

When you get a cold or a sniffle, use a handkerchief and not a tissue.

32 Read your garbage

Learn the recycling symbols and make sure you're recycling as much as you can.

33 Carry on shopping

The next time you go shopping, use a cloth bag or an old plastic bag.

34 One in, one out

Make someone's day. When you get a new toy, give an old one away.

35 Take care

Look after your things. The fewer things you break, the fewer new things you need.

36 Buy second-hand stuff

It helps reduce waste and means new things don't need to be made.

37 Learn to fix things

Try fixing something that's broken instead of replacing it.

Want more ideas for reusing things? Go to ideas 54 to 58.

38 MAKE A MONSTROUS SOCK

Quite a lot of what we throw away is actually stuff that could be reused or turned into something else. But not everything you make has to be useful. You can make fun things using old stuff too!

How can sock monsters save the world?

They can't do it by themselves—they're not superheroes! But you can put your old socks to good use.

You will need:

- 1 sock
- stuffing (old fabric cut up)
- scissors, needle, and thread
- 2 buttons
- an adult to help you

2. Cut down from the toe to make two ears. Sew along the edge of the ears.

1. Turn your sock inside out with the heel facing up.

Top Tip!
Ask a grown-up before you start cutting things up.

3. Turn your sock the right way out, put stuffing in it, and then sew up the bottom.

39 Brilliant birthday cards
Cover old cards with pictures from magazines, then write your own message inside.

40 Sleepy shopping bag
Add handles to an old pillowcase and make a bag. Decorate it with old buttons or fabric.

41 Old is new
Instead of throwing out old clothes, why not alter them to the style you want?

42 Reuse your old jeans
Use the leg of old jeans as door draft stoppers. Cut off a jean leg, stuff it with old fabric or plastic bags, and sew up both ends.

43 Jam jar holders
Jam jars can hold pens, pennies, and much more.

44 Think outside the box
Why don't you look at your garbage and think of new ways to reuse it?

4. Sew on the buttons to make eyes.

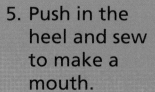

5. Push in the heel and sew to make a mouth.

45 SEE THE WORLD BY BIKE!

Every time you get in a car to go somewhere, you add to global warming. That's because car engines release a greenhouse gas called carbon dioxide. So, one good way to save the world is . . . to stop being driven around in cars!

Bring on the bike

Bikes are *way* better than cars, for loads of reasons. The main reason is that they don't let out greenhouse gases. Oh, and they don't get stuck in traffic jams either!

A bike can take you practically everywhere. The next time you plan to go somewhere, think "Can I go by bike?"

Top Tip!

Remember to wear a helmet and make sure your mom or dad knows where you are going.

46 Use human power

If you don't have a bike, how about skateboarding, walking, or rollerblading?

47 Hop on the train or bus

If it's raining, go by train or bus. They burn less fossil fuel per passenger than cars.

48 The walking bus

Ask your school to start a walking bus if you can't cycle to school.

49 Give someone a lift

If you and your friend are going to the same place, get your mom or dad to give your friend a ride. That means only one car makes the trip, not two.

50 Roll up the windows

If you *do* travel by car, try not to open the windows too much. Cars run better with the windows closed.

51 Go slow

On long car journeys, ask the driver to travel at 55–65 mph. Most cars use less fuel at this speed.

52 Plan a day out

The next time you plan a family trip, go somewhere you can get to by train, by bus, or on foot.

53 LOVE A LIBRARY

Help save the world by reading books! As long as they're not brand-new copies, that is. Instead, get them from a library. That way fewer books need to be made!

Recycling paper is good . . .

Much of the recycling from people's homes is paper. It comes from books, newspapers, magazines, and **packaging**. It's all taken away and turned into new paper. Recycled paper is much better for the planet than non-recycled paper.

. . . but using less paper is better.

Even recycled paper harms the planet. Making it still produces **pollution** and adds to global warming. So, wherever possible, try to use less paper.

54 Double it
Use the backs of sheets of paper, not just the front.

55 Start a book group
Share books with your friends, especially this book!

56 Perfect pad
Make your own scrap-paper pad. Use it for notes and messages.

57 Reuse newspapers
Make your own paper plates. Tear up old newspapers and soak them in water. Then press the paper onto a plate and wait for it to dry. Perfect for using for more craft activities.

58 New ideas
While you're riding the bus to the library (see idea 47), maybe you can come up with some other paper-related ways to save the world!

59 BE A ROLE MODEL

Many people come from a time when no one really bothered much about saving the world. This is not their fault—hardly anyone knew back then that the world *needed* saving!

How can I make a difference?

You *are* different. You have lots of ideas about saving the world. Don't be selfish—share what you know. After all, lots of people acting in the same way can make things a *lot* better.

Spread the word

Why not start with your school? Think about the things you would like to do differently. Speak to your classmates and teachers. Can you spread the word and make a difference?

FAST FACT
When **Earth Day** was first celebrated on April 22, 1970, just one country took part. By 2010, it was celebrated by 175 countries.

Top Tip!
Remember to ask before changing anything at school.

SAVE THE WORLD TODAY

I would like:

- ○ more places to put bikes
- ○ monthly trading of clothes and toys
- ○ recycling bins in every class
- ○ walking buses
- ○ a "Get to school without a car" day

60 Hold a waste test
Ask if you can monitor the school's bins before they're collected. Could you reduce the amount of garbage?

61 Celebrate!
Why not get your school to celebrate Earth Day?

62 Get sponsored
Do a sponsored walk, swim, or cycle for an environmental charity.

63 Be a green author
Make a "green" book, like this one, explaining to other children what they can do to help save the world.

64 Change a friend
Don't switch friends! Just persuade one friend to do an activity from this book.

65 Look back
Go through the book. Which activities can you do at school?

66 Green days
Start a "green" diary. Record all the things you do to help save the world.

One day a cavewoman looked at her husband dragging a load of firewood back to their cave. "I wonder if there's a better way of doing that?" she thought. A week later—hey, presto! Wheels!

How can we change things?

Things only change when someone wonders why things are the way they are—and whether they could be better. Great news: you've already started to think differently by reading this book!

Things only change when someone wonders …

Why not keep a note of your questions in your green diary? See idea 66.

68

Ask it!
What question will
you ask today?

... Why things are
the way they are.

GLOSSARY

atmosphere layer of gases surrounding a planet

Earth Day chosen day every year for people to think about looking after Earth

food chain series of plants and animals in which each one serves as food for the next in the chain

fossil fuels energy resources formed from the remains of plants and animals from millions of years ago, which will eventually run out

global warming increase in the temperature of Earth, which may change weather patterns and affect plants, wildlife, and people

greenhouse gases gases that cause global warming

packaging wrapping that goes around things we buy

pollution materials that cause harm to the natural world

INDEX

car travel 16–17

clothes 6–7

cycling 16

Earth Day 20, 21

energy, saving 8, 10–11

food chain 4

garbage 5, 12–13, 15, 21

global warming 2, 8, 10, 16, 18

greenhouse gases 2, 5, 6, 8, 10, 16

growing plants 5

heating, turning down 8–9

libraries 18–19

nature areas 5

paper, saving 18–19

reduce, reuse, recycle 12–15, 18–19

resources 3

sock monsters 14–15

spiders 4

spreading the word 20–21

swapping and giving away 7, 13

travel 16–17

warm, keeping 8–9